# TRIVIA FOR SENIORS

## NANCY MACQUILKEN

For additional copies contact:

Commonwealth Legacy

www.commonwealthlegacy.com

www.triviaforseniors.com

Email: bosocala@yahoo.com

ISBN 13: 978-0615452425

In Memory of June E. Burton

This book is dedicated to the residents of the William B. Rice Eventide Home. Thank you for sharing your interest in trivia. I'd like to name a few ladies who helped me get started with the trivia program. Marcella Serafini, Mary English, Laura Lynch, Margaret Hamill, Ruth Gordon, Helen Ferrigno and my mom June Burton. It was their enthusiasm that was the driving force behind this trivia book.

# Categories

History

Animals

Famous People

Geography

Sports

Common Bonds

Entertainment

Potpourri

Bible

# History

1-Who is the only U.S. President buried in Washington's National Cathedral?

Woodrow Wilson

2-Who was Chiang Kai Shek?

Leader of the Republic of China 1949-1975

3-Who was Robert E. Lee?

Confederate General

4-Who was Nelson Rockefeller?

Governor of New York 1959-1973 Vice President under President Ford 1974-1977

5-Who was Elizabeth Cady Stanton?

An American reformer and leader of the women's suffrage movement

6-Who was the first woman appointed to the U.S. Supreme Court?

Sandra Day O'Connor

7-During World War II these terms were used—what do they mean?

VJ Day-----------Victory in Japan

VE Day----------Victory in Europe

8-What were the names of the ships that brought Christopher Columbus to the new world?

Nina   Pinta   Santa Maria

9-Who was the Queen that financed Columbus' voyage?

Queen Isabella of Spain

10-Name the children of Queen Elizabeth II

Charles, Anne, Andrew, Edward

11-Which U.S. President served the most consecutive terms?

Franklin Delano Roosevelt

12-What is the name of the ship that carried the Pilgrims to America?

Mayflower

13-Where did the Pilgrims land?

Plymouth, Massachusetts

14-What are the first ten amendments to the constitution called and what is their purpose?

The Bill of Rights—they were created to protect the rights of citizens against oppression by the government

15-Who designed the Eiffel Tower and what was the event it was built for?

Gustave Eiffel in 1889 for the World's Fair in Paris

16-What was Paul Revere's occupation?

Silversmith-he made tankards, bowls, pitchers, tea sets

17-Where did the famous "Tea Party" occur in 1773?

Boston Harbor

18-You have to be at least how old to be elected U.S. President?

35 years old

19-Who invented the cotton gin?

Eli Whitney

20-What U.S. President was born on the 4th of July 1872?

Calvin Coolidge-born in Plymouth Vermont

21-Which U.S. state gave women the right to vote in 1869?

Wyoming

22-Who invented the telephone?

Alexander Graham Bell

23-What type of work did George Washington do as a young man?

Surveyor

24-What did the U.S. Congress adopt in 1918 (during W.W.I) to save coal and electricity?

Daylight savings time

25-What conservative and pro family politician was the only divorced man to serve as U.S. President?

Ronald Reagan

26-Which two presidential candidates were in the 1960 debate?

John Kennedy and Richard Nixon

27-What is the most common first name for U.S. Presidents?

James (Madison, Monroe, Polk, Buchanan, Garfield, Carter)

28-What does the U.S. President place his hand on while taking the oath of office?

Bible

29-Which president's home can be seen from the Potomac River?

George Washington

30-Which two presidents died on the same day, July 4, 1826?

John Adams and Thomas Jefferson

31-Who was the youngest U.S. President to serve?

Teddy Roosevelt-William McKinley was assassinated –Roosevelt succeeded him.

John F. Kennedy was the youngest U.S. President to be elected

32-What statue in New York City did President Grover Cleveland officially dedicate in 1886?

Statue of Liberty

33-A sign reading, "The Buck Stops Here", was found on which 20th century president's desk?

Harry S. Truman

34-In 1912 Japan gave the United States what type of tree as a gift of friendship?

Cherry Tree

35-Who is the only U.S. President never to have been elected either president or vice-president?

Gerald Ford-he was appointed vice-president to replace Spiro Agnew-then Nixon had to resign

36-What republican First Lady was known as the "Silver Fox"?

Barbara Bush

37-What First Lady did not have to change her last name when she married?

Eleanor Roosevelt-Franklin was her cousin

38-Who was the first U.S. President to refer to his D.C. home as the White House?

Teddy Roosevelt-in 1901-1902 he had it printed on the stationary and also issued a

Proclamation-until that time the house had been referred to as the President's House or the Executive Mansion.

39-First Lady Claudia Alta Taylor Johnson was better known by what name?

Lady Bird Johnson

40-Independence Missouri was the hometown of which 20th century president?

Harry S. Truman

41-What was President Harry Truman's middle name?

S—only the letter

42-Which U.S. President gave the shortest inaugural speech-only 134 words?

George Washington

43-When George Washington was inaugurated in 1789 what city was the U.S. capital?

New York City

44-On the eve of the Great Depression, which presidential candidate promised "a chicken in every pot"?

Herbert Hoover

45-What First Lady took television viewers on a White House tour on Valentine's Day 1962?

Jackie Kennedy

46-What Republican President of the 1980's bluntly called the Soviet Union, "An evil empire"?

Ronald Reagan

47-In Boone Iowa you can visit the birthplace of which First Lady of the 1950's?

Mamie Eisenhower

48-What President gave the longest inaugural speech and then had the shortest term?

William Henry Harrison-8445 words and his term only lasted 32 days. He died of pneumonia

49-Who was the only bachelor President?

James Buchanan –he was engaged to Ann Coleman-she broke the engagement and died shortly after

50-President Rutherford B. Hayes's wife was nicknamed "Lemonade Lucy" because she refused to serve what in the White House?

Alcohol

51-Lyndon Johnson was how many cars behind President John Kennedy when Kennedy was shot?

Three

52-In 1914 President Wilson designated what holiday as the second Sunday in May?

Mother's Day

53-Which state contributed a President to each side of the Civil War?

Kentucky –birthplace of both Abraham Lincoln and Jefferson Davis

54-Margaret Thatcher was the first woman Prime Minister of what country?

England

55-What country was Pope John Paul II from?

Poland

56-What U.S. President gave Fireside Chats?

Franklin Roosevelt

57-Who was Charles DeGaulle?

President of France

58-Who was Winston Churchill?

Prime Minister of England

59-Who signed the Social Security Act into law?

President Franklin Roosevelt

60-What state was the Lindberg baby kidnapped from?

New Jersey-Hopewell

61-In what New York city was President McKinley assassinated?

Buffalo

62-What country gave the Statue of Liberty to the U.S.?

France

63-Which 4 U.S. Presidents are on Mt. Rushmore?

Washington, Jefferson, Lincoln, Teddy Roosevelt

64-What was the Manhattan Project?

A United States project to develop the Atomic Bomb

65-Who was Douglas MacArthur?

A Five Star General and commander of the Allied Forces in the Southwest Pacific during W.W.II

66-What was the Cocoanut Grove and what incident occurred there in 1942?

It was a night club in Boston--- in 1942 a fire there killed 492 people

67-Who was Yasser Arafat?

President of the Palestinian Authority

68-What was the Tennessee Valley Authority?

A jobs program that was started during the Great Depression to create jobs and develop the natural resources of the Tennessee River Basin

69-In what city did the famous Brink's Robbery of 1950 occur?

Boston

70-Who were Bonnie and Clyde?

Robbers

71-What U.S. President had a domestic policy called the "Great Society"?

Lyndon Johnson

72-How many U.S. Presidents have been assassinated?

Four

73-Name the U.S. Presidents that have been assassinated

Abraham Lincoln, James Garfield, William McKinley, John Kennedy

74-Under which U.S. President did the Bay of Pigs occur?

John F. Kennedy

75-Which President was in office when the Great Depression started?

Herbert Hoover

76-Who was the oldest man elected to be president?

Ronald Reagan

77-Which car built in 1903 was purchased for $850?

Ford –Model A

78-What was George Washington's wife name?

Martha

79-What was the name of George Washington's home?

Mount Vernon

80-Who is the only President to have a state named after him?

George Washington

81-Who was Bruno Hauptmann?

Man convicted of kidnapping the Lindbergh baby

82-Who was Albert DeSalvo?

Accused of being the Boston Strangler

83-Who was Betsy Ross?

A seamstress from American Revolution times-said to have made the first U.S. flag

84-Who was the first female U.S. Attorney General?

Janet Reno

85-Where is Buckingham Palace and who lives there?

London England-the British Monarch

86-What was the U.S. war between the north and south called?

Civil War

87-In the U.S. line of succession who is next in line after the President?

Vice President

88-In what state was John Kennedy assassinated?

Texas

89-Which President had a pet alligator?

John Quincy Adams

90-Which two U.S. Presidents are buried in Arlington National Cemetery?

William Howard Taft and John F. Kennedy

91-Hillary Clinton was a U. S. Senator from which state?

New York

92-Who was the leader of the Nazi's from 1933-1945?

Adolf Hitler

93-Who was the tallest President?

Abraham Lincoln-6'4"

94-Who was the shortest President?

James Madison-5'4"

95-What war took place while Lincoln was President?

Civil War

96-How did Lincoln die?

Shot by John Wilkes Booth

97-How many brothers did John F. Kennedy have?

Three- Bobby, Ted, Joseph

98-What does the F stand for in John F. Kennedy?

Fitzgerald

99-Where was the first U.S. public beach?

Revere Beach Massachusetts -1896

100-Who was Joan of Arc?

A French heroine of the Hundred Years War against England

101-When did these happen?

The bombing of Pearl Harbor

December 7, 1941

The Battle of Gettysburg

July 1863

The crash of the stock market

October 1929

The first man on the moon

July 1969

102-What is the name of the Massachusetts Governor who ran for President in 1988?

Michael Dukakis

103-Who was Dukakis's running mate?

Lloyd Benson

104-Who was Tip O'Neil?

Speaker of the U.S. House of Representatives

105-Who is Ed Koch?

Former Mayor of New York City

106-Which U.S. President liked to eat jelly beans?

Ronald Reagan

107-What is the oldest commissioned floating vessel in the world?

U.S.S. Constitution –Old Ironsides

108-Who was the first catholic elected U.S. President?

John Kennedy

109-Which U.S. President was in office when the stock market crashed in 1929?

Herbert Hoover

110-In what U.S. city is the Liberty Bell?

Philadelphia

111-In what state did Paul Revere make his famous ride?

Massachusetts April 18, 1775

112-What was the pony express?

Mail delivery service

113-What Egyptian woman was known as Queen of the Nile?

Cleopatra

114-What U. S. President died at Dallas' Parkland Hospital November 22, 1963?

John Kennedy

115-June 14 is what U.S. holiday?

Flag Day

116-What Washington D.C. structure is 550 feet tall?

Washington Monument

117-How many U.S. Senators are elected from each state?

Two

118-What are the first ten amendments to the U.S. Constitution called?

Bill of Rights

119-In what U.S. state was Bill Clinton born?

Arkansas

120-How did John Kennedy Jr. die?

A plane crash

121-"Live Free of Die", is the motto of which state?

New Hampshire

122-In what state was Jimmy Carter born?

Georgia

123-What was Barbara Bush's dog's name?

Millie

124-What was Bill Clinton's dog's name?

Buddy

125-What was Ronald Reagan's first wife's name?

Jane Wyman

126-Who was the President during the Watergate scandal?

Nixon

127-Former Vice President Spiro Agnew resigned from office due to what legal problem?

Tax evasion

128-How many Supreme Court Justices are there?

Nine

129-How many U. S. Senators are there?

One hundred

130-What is the name of the President's office?

Oval Office

131-What were the last two states to join the Union?

Alaska (49th) Hawaii (50th) both in 1959

132-Huey Long was the Governor from which state?

Louisiana

133-How long is the U.S. President's term?

Four years

134-What are George W. Bush's daughter's names?

Jenna & Barbara

135-Who was Ethan Allen?

He led the Green Mountain Boys during the Revolutionary War

136-What religion is Mitt Romney?

Mormon

137-What is Hamas?

Militant Palestinian Islamic movement

138-Where would you find the Khmer Rouge?

Cambodia

139-What was prohibition?

Banning the manufacture, sale & transportation of alcohol

140-During the Revolutionary War the British soldiers were referred to by what nickname?

Redcoats

141-Where was the first hostile action during the Civil War?

Fort Sumter

142-In 1540 what explorer was looking for the "Seven Cities of Gold"?

Francisco Coronado

143-Which of Henry VIII wives gave birth to Elizabeth I?

Ann Boleyn

144-What disgraced Vice President's high school yearbook quote read: "an ounce of wit is worth a pound of sorrow"?

Spiro Agnew

145-What was the first country to recognize Mexico's independence in 1836?

United States

146-Princess Diana and Prince Charles had two sons-what are their names?

William & Harry

# Animals

1-What kind of bear lives in the Arctic?

Polar bear

2-What kind of animal is a python?

Snake

3-What kind of animal is a koala?

Bear

4-What is blubber?

Thick layer of fatty tissue located between muscle and skin of marine mammals

5-What is a female lion called?

Lioness

6-What animal builds a dam?

Beaver

7-Why do woodpeckers peck wood?

To find insects, to make nests, to signal other birds

8-What insect transmits the bubonic plague?

Flea

9-Which part of the bee makes the buzzing sound?

Wings

10-What are beaver's homes called?

Dam or lodge

11-What animal has a long neck and long legs?

Giraffe

12-What animal has needle like quills on its body?

Porcupine

13-What animal is called king of the beasts?

Lion

14-What type of animal is a boa constrictor?

Snake

15-From what animals do you get ivory?

Elephant & walrus

16-What is a young dog called?

Puppy

17-What does a tadpole grow up to be?

Frog

18-What animal carries a jockey?

Horse

19-What type of animal was Moby Dick?

Sperm whale

20-What is a female deer called?

Doe or hind

21-What is a male deer called?

Buck or stag

22-What is a baby deer called?

Fawn

23-What is a baby seal called?

Pup

24-Which bird is the fastest swimmer?

Gentoo penguin

25-What is a baby horse called?

Foal

26-What does a caterpillar change into?

Butterfly

27-What is a baby cat called?

Kitten

28-Does the male or the female mosquito bite?

Female

29-What color is a panda bear?

Black and white

30-What does a camel store in his hump?

Excess fat

31-What is a palomino?

A horse of a golden color with a white mane

32-What large furry animal sleeps throughout the winter?

Bear

33-What do squirrels collect in the fall for the wintertime?

Nuts

34-What is a daddy longlegs?

Spider

35-Do fish have scales or quills?

Scales

36-What type of animal is a Holstein?

Cow

37-What type of animal is a Clydesdale?

Horse

38-What type of animal is a collie?

Dog

39-What is the first animal listed in the dictionary?

Aardvark

40-What swimming stroke is named after an insect?

Butterfly

41-What unit of measurement is used to measure a horse's height?

Hands-one hand equals 4 inches

42-What kind of bird can dive the deepest below sea level (about 500 meters underwater)?

Emperor penguin

43-What big cat cannot retract its claws?

Cheetah

44-Where do flies go in the winter?

Diapause (sort of hibernation-but they do not grow) they go to dry & warm spaces

# Famous People

1-Who was Vincent Van Gogh?

Dutch Post Impressionist painter

2-Who was Karl Marx?

German social philosopher and chief theorist of socialism-- he wrote <u>Das</u> <u>Capital</u>

3-Who was J. Edgar Hoover?

Director of the F.B.I. (1924-1972)

4-Who was Charles Dickens?

British author

5-Who is Spiro Agnew?

Vice president under Richard Nixon (resigned after being accused of accepting bribes)

6-Who was Pablo Picasso?

Spanish artist and sculptor

7-Who was Robert Frost?

American poet

8-Who was Jimmy Hoffa?

President of the Teamsters Union

9-Who was Francis Scott Key?

United States lawyer & poet-he wrote "The Star Spangled Banner"

10-What is Queen Elizabeth's only daughter's name?

Princess Anne

11-Who wrote the Pulitzer Prize winning novel <u>The</u> <u>Color</u> <u>Purple</u>?

Alice Walker

12-Who was Henry Ford?

American founder of the Ford motor company and adopted the assembly line for cars

13-Who was Walt Whitman?

American poet

14-Who was Michelangelo?

Italian Renaissance painter

15-Who are the three "B's" of classical music?

Brahms, Beethoven, Bach

16-Who was William Tecumseh Sherman?

Civil War general

17-Who invented air brakes?

George Westinghouse in 1868

18-Where did the concept of ambulance service start?

In Europe with the Knights of St. John

19-Who designed St. Paul's Cathedral of London?

Sir Christopher Wren

20-Who wrote Uncle Tom's Cabin?

Harriet Beecher Stowe

21-Who wrote Pride and Prejudice?

Jane Austin

22-Who was known as the March King?

John Philip Sousa

23-Who is Sirhan Sirhan?

He assassinated Robert Kennedy

24-What was Robert Kennedy's middle initial?

F (Francis)

25-What former football player wrestled Sirhan Sirhan to the floor after the shooting of Robert Kennedy?

Rosey Grier

26-Who were the Wright brothers?

The first to fly a powered plane

27-What were the Wright brothers' first names?

Orville and Wilbur

28-Who was Agatha Christie?

Writer of crime novels

29-Who is Shirley Temple?

Child actress who as an adult became an Ambassador to Ghana and Czechoslovakia

30-Who was Al Capone?

Gangster-during the prohibition era

31-Who were Rogers and Hammerstein?

American songwriters

32-Who was Colonel Sanders?

The founder of Kentucky Fried Chicken

33-Who invented the Barbie doll?

Ruth Handler in 1959

34-Who was Jacques Cousteau?

Undersea explorer

35-Who was Bruno Hauptmann?

Convicted of kidnapping the Lindberg baby in 1932

36-Who is Ruth Bader Ginsburg?

Second woman to sit on the U.S. Supreme Court

37-Who was John Hancock?

Political leader during the Revolutionary War

38-Who was Dwight Eisenhower?

American General during WWII and 34th President of the United States

39-Who was Norman Rockwell?

American illustrator-known for his covers of the Saturday Evening Post

40-Who was Ray Kroc?

Builder of McDonald's fast food empire

41-Who is Mario Cuomo?

Former governor of New York

42-Who is Patty Hearst?

Newspaper heiress and a kidnap victim from the 1970's

43-Who is John McCain?

U.S. Senator from Arizona

44-Who is Ralph Nader?

Consumer advocate and presidential candidate

45-Who was Mark Twain?

An American author & humorist-born Samuel Langhorne Clemens

46-Who was Lizzie Borden?

A Fall River, Ma woman accused of killing her father and stepmother

47-Who is Eric Holder?

Attorney General under President Barack Obama

48-Who is Ed Koch?

Former Mayor of New York City

49-Who was Frank Lloyd Wright?

Architect

50-Who was the first Secretary of the Department of Homeland Security?

Tom Ridge

51-Who was Muddy Waters?

A musician-he helped create the Chicago Blues sound in the 1940's

52-Who was Amelia Earhart?

Aviation pioneer

53-Who was Benazir Bhutto?

Prime Minister of Pakistan-assassinated December 2007

54-Who was Charles Atlas?

Bodybuilder

55-Who was Charles Bulfinch?

American Architect

56-Who was the founder of the Rainbow Coalition?

Jesse Jackson

57-Who was Grandma Moses?

American folk artist-started painting in her seventies

58-Who are Bob Woodward and Carl Bernstein?

Journalists for the Washington Post who uncovered the Watergate Scandal

59-Who was Clara Barton?

Founder of the American Red Cross

60-Who was Paul Gauguin?

French artist

61-Who was Nathan Hale?

American patriot of the American Revolution

62-Who was Martin Luther King?

Civil rights leader

63-Who was Anne Frank?

A young girl of German-Dutch ancestry who wrote her experiences during W.W.II in the book The Diary of Anne Frank

64-Who was Margaret Mitchell?

Author of Gone with the Wind

65-Who was Pearl Buck?

An American author who wrote of her life in China, her parents were missionaries

66-Who was Annie Oakley?

An American sharpshooter and entertainer

67-Who was Bobby Fischer?

An American champion chess player

68-Who was Rosa Parks?

A black woman who refused to give up her bus seat to a white man in 1955

69-Who was Geronimo?

An Apache chief born in Arizona in 1829

70-Who was Johnny Weissmuller?

An Olympic gold medal winning swimmer, actor that played Tarzan

71-Who was Davy Crockett?

An American frontiersman, soldier, politician

72-Who was Samuel Colt?

Inventor of the revolver

73-Who was the author of Poor Richard's Almanac?

Ben Franklin

74-Who wrote the Star Spangled Banner?

Francis Scott Key

75-Who invented the phonograph?

Thomas Edison

76-Who invented the lightening rod?

Benjamin Franklin

77-Who wrote Rip Van Winkle?

Washington Irving

78-Who was George Pullman?

An American inventor-he invented the Pullman sleeping car

79-Who was the author of The Raven?

Edgar Allan Poe

80-Who invented the steamboat?

Robert Fulton

81-Who wrote Moby Dick?

Herman Melville

82-Who wrote The Man without a Country?

Edward Everett Hale

83-Who was Samuel Morse?

Inventor of the telegraph

84-Who wrote Little Women?

Louisa May Alcott

85-Who was George Eastman?

Inventor of the roll film

86-Who wrote The Adventures of Tom Sawyer?

Mark Twain

87-What type of books did Zane Gray write?

Westerns

88-Henry and Richard Block founded what company in 1956?

H & R Block –income tax preparers

89-Until Chet Huntley retired in 1970, who was his co-anchor on NBC News?

David Brinkley

90-What two famous English preachers are connected with colonial Georgia?

John and Charles Wesley

91-What naval hero is buried in the Chapel of the U.S. Naval Academy?

John Paul Jones

92-What female Massachusetts poet's home can be visited in Amherst?

Emily Dickinson

93-Who was Audie Murphy?

An actor who was the most decorated American combat soldier in W.W. II

94-Who was Eugene O'Neill?

A Pulitzer Prize winning American playwright

95-Who was Georgia O'Keefe?

An American artist

96-What was President Buchanan's home named?

Wheatland

97-What was President Jackson's home named?

Hermitage

98-What was Andrew Jackson's nickname?

Old Hickory

99-What was President Madison's home named?

Montpelier

100-What was President Monroe's home named?

Ash Lawn-Highland

# Geography

1-What countries make up the British Isles?

Ireland, Wales, Scotland, England

2-What is the capital of Northern Ireland?

Belfast

3-What is the capital of the Republic of Ireland?

Dublin

4-What is the capital of Wales?

Cardiff

5-What is the capital of Scotland?

Edinburgh

6-Name 4 states that begin with the letter W

Wyoming, West Virginia, Wisconsin, Washington

7-Name 2 states that begin with the letter T

Texas, Tennessee

8-What is the only U.S. state with an area of less than 2 thousand square miles?

Rhode Island

9-Canada lies south of the United States at only 1 point, near what Michigan city

Detroit

10-What is the only U.S. state to border only one other state?

Maine

11-What two U.S. states do not border any other state?

Alaska & Hawaii

12-The United States largest maritime museum is in Mystic Seaport in which New England state?

Connecticut

13-What U.S. state capital is closest to the equator?

Honolulu, Hawaii

14-What U.S. city is the country music capital?

Nashville, Tennessee

15-What 2 countries share Niagara Falls?

United States -- Canada

16-In what U.S. harbor is the Statue of Liberty?

New York

17-What 3 U.S. states begin & end with the letter A?

Alabama, Alaska & Arizona

18-Name the 7 continents

Europe, North America, South America, Asia, Africa, Australia, Antarctica

19-Which of the 7 continents has the most countries?

Africa

20-Warsaw is located in what European country?

Poland

21-In what European city would you find the Eiffel Tower?

Paris

22-What is the largest U.S. state?

Alaska

23-In what country is the man made waterway that links the Atlantic Ocean and the Pacific Ocean?

Panama

24-In what country would you find Windsor Castle?

England

25-What European country is shaped like a boot?

Italy

26-In what U.S. city would you find the Old North Church, Faneuil Hall and the Freedom Trail?

Boston

27-What European city is called the Eternal City?

Rome

28-The 630 ft. tall St. Louis gateway arch rises alongside the Mississippi River in what U.S. state?

Missouri

29-What New England state does not touch the ocean?

Vermont

30-In what European city would you hear Big Ben sounding the hour?

London (Parliament)

31-Times Square is in what U.S. city?

New York

32-In what country is the Great Wall?

China

33-What country is also a continent?

Australia

34-The Appian Way, first paved with stones in 321 B.C. was a major road into what European capital?

Rome

35-What city is the capital of Japan?

Tokyo

36-What city in Louisiana is known for Mardi Gras celebrations?

New Orleans

37-The cities of Rio de Janeiro, Buenos Aires, Lima, and Caracas are located on what continent?

South America

38-What is the world's smallest country?

Vatican City

39-New Hampshire's largest city is named after an industrial city in England

Name the city

Manchester

40-What U.S. state produces the most potatoes?

Idaho

41-Through what European city does the Thames River flow?

London

42-In what two U.S. states are the Great Smokey Mountains?

Tennessee --North Carolina

43-What is the longest river in New England?

Connecticut River

44-What U.S. state is the smallest?

Rhode Island

45-What is the only continent that is covered by an ice cap?

Antarctica

46-What state nicknamed the Green Mountain State, has the words, Freedom and Unity as its motto?

Vermont

47-What is the largest lake west of the Mississippi River?

Great Salt Lake

48-Name the 5 Great Lakes

Superior, Michigan, Huron, Erie, Ontario

49-In what country do sheep out number people 20 to 1?

New Zealand

50-What country is called the Emerald Isle?

Ireland

51-What two U.S. states have 8 states on their borders?

Tennessee-- Missouri

52-Name the 8 states bordering Tennessee.

Mississippi, Arkansas, Alabama, Georgia, North Carolina, Virginia, Kentucky, Missouri

53-Name the 8 states bordering Missouri.

Tennessee, Kentucky, Illinois, Iowa, Nebraska, Kansas, Oklahoma, Arkansas

54-In what U.S. city is the Alamo located?

San Antonio

55-Name the U.S. states that are located on the Gulf of Mexico.

Florida, Alabama, Louisiana, Mississippi, Texas

56-What U.S. state is bordered by 4 Great Lakes?

Michigan

57-What U.S. state would you be in if you were swimming in the Great Salt Lake?

Utah

58-Name the U.S. state that begins with the letter R

Rhode Island

59-What is the largest country in North America?

Canada

60-Name 4 U.S. states that begin with the word "New"

New York, New Jersey, New Mexico, New Hampshire

61-Name 3 U.S. states that begin with the letter C

Connecticut, California, Colorado

62-What was the name of Liberty Island in New York Bay before the Statue of Liberty was constructed?

Bedloe's Island-name was changed in 1956

63-What land locked state contains the largest saltwater body of water in the United States?

Utah-The Great Salt Lake

64-What historic New England capital celebrates Bunker Hill Day each June?

Boston

65-What U. S. state would you be in if you were visiting Atlantic City?

New Jersey

66-What U.S. state is bordered by the Atlantic Ocean and the Gulf of Mexico?

Florida

67-Name 2 U.S. states that begin with the letter S

South Carolina, South Dakota

68-Name four states that begin with the letter I

Idaho, Indiana, Illinois, Iowa

69-What is the name of the large mountain range in the western United States?

Rocky Mountains

70-Name the U.S. states that begin with the letter K

Kentucky, Kansas

71-What U.S. state named its capital after Abraham Lincoln?

Nebraska

72-What is the name of the large mountain range in the eastern U.S.?

Appalachian Mountains

73-In what state would you find Mt. Washington?

New Hampshire

74-What state capital is named after the 3rd President of the United States?

Jefferson City, Missouri

75-What is Niagara Falls and where is it?

Waterfall-located in both upstate New York and Canada- separated by Goat Island

76-Identify these U.S. cities:

City of Angels—Los Angeles

City of Brotherly Love—Philadelphia

Windy City—Chicago

Motor City—Detroit

Beantown—Boston

77-In what U.S. city is Disney World?

Orlando, Florida

78-In what U.S. city is the Empire State Building?

New York City

79-In what U.S. city is the Sears Tower?

Chicago

80-In what U.S. city is Disneyland?

Anaheim, California

81-In what European city would you find Regent Street & Kensington Gardens?

London

82-In what European city would you find the Champs Elysees and the Tuileries?

Paris

83-In what U.S. city would you find Market Street and Golden Gate Park?

San Francisco

84-In what U.S. city would you find the Mercantile Mart?

Chicago

85-Identify these U.S. states

The Last Frontier—Alaska

The Lone Star State—Texas

The Blue Grass State—Kentucky

The Aloha State—Hawaii

The Constitution State—Connecticut

The Green Mountain State—Vermont

The Hoosier State—Indiana

The Grand Canyon State—Arizona

The Bay State—Massachusetts

The Palmetto State—South Carolina

The First State—Delaware

The Keystone State—Pennsylvania

The Golden State—California

The Ocean State—Rhode Island

The Peach State—Georgia

The Granite State—New Hampshire

The Show Me State—Missouri

The Pelican State—Louisiana

The Sunflower State—Kansas

86-In what U.S. state would you find?

Death Valley—California

Sun Valley—Idaho

Badlands—South Dakota

Painted Desert—Arizona

Carlsbad Caverns—New Mexico

Pike's Peak—Colorado

Lake Tahoe—Nevada

Mt. Rushmore—South Dakota (Black Hills)

87-Where would you find Martha's Vineyard & Nantucket?

Off the coast of Cape Cod Massachusetts

88-What was Alcatraz and where is it?

A prison off the coast of San Francisco

89-Where is Staten Island?

New York Harbor

90-Where would you find the Kremlin?

Moscow

91-Where is Stonehenge?

England

92-Where is the Taj Mahal?

Agra, India.

93-Where is the Doge's Palace?

Venice

94-In what country is the Sydney Opera House?

Australia

95-What is the saltiest body of water on Earth?

Dead Sea-located between Israel & Jordan

96-Name all six New England states

Massachusetts, New Hampshire, Vermont, Rhode Island, Connecticut, Maine

97-In what New England state is Nashua located?

New Hampshire

98-What New England state is referred to as the insurance capital?

Connecticut

99-In which New England state is Mt. Desert Island located?

Maine

100-What is the highest point in the United States?

Mt. McKinley at 6,198 miles

101-What is the lowest point in the United States?

Death Valley in California

102-Where is Camp David?

Maryland-it's a retreat for U.S. Presidents

103-Where is Rio de Janeiro?

Brazil

104-Where is Barcelona?

Spain

105-Where is Cape Town?

South Africa

106-Where is Versailles?

France

107-Where is Quebec?

Canada

108-In what state is the Redwood National Park?

California

109-In what country is the city of Nagasaki located?

Japan

110-In what country is the city of Dresden located?

Germany

111-In what city is the Louvre Museum located?

Paris

112-In what city is the Guggenheim Museum located?

New York

113-On what body of water is the principality of Monaco located?

Mediterranean Sea

114-What river did the original London Bridge span?

Thames River

115-What is the capital of Ohio?

Columbus

116-What is the name of the river that separates Arizona & California?

Colorado River

117-What island city was the site of an attack December 7, 1941?

Honolulu, Hawaii

118-In what state would you find Key West?

Florida

119-What country did the United States buy Alaska from?

Russia

120-What is the name of the river between Texas & Mexico?

Rio Grande

121-Name two Pennsylvania cities that begin with the letter P

Pittsburgh, Philadelphia

122-What is Italy's longest river?

Po

123-What is the longest river in France?

Loire

124-What is the longest river in the United States?

Missouri—2,540 miles long

125-Name 3 Pacific Coast states

California, Oregon & Washington

126-What is the Delmarva Peninsula?

A large peninsula on the east coast of the United States, occupied by Delaware, and portions of Maryland and Virginia

127-Where is Chesapeake Bay?

An inlet of the Atlantic Ocean, separating the Delmarva Peninsula from mainland Maryland and Virginia

128-Name 3 states that touch California

Arizona, Nevada, Oregon

129-In what European country is the Black Forest?

Germany

130-What is Maryland's state capital?

Annapolis

131-What is New York's state flower?

Rose

132-What is Delaware's capital?

Dover

133-What is California's state tree?

Redwood

134-What is Alaska's state flower?

Forget me not

135-What is Washington's state tree?

Western Hemlock

136-What state name only has 1 syllable?

Maine

137-Where is Caracas?

Venezuela

138-Where is the Amazon River?

South America

139-Where is the United Nations located?

New York City

140-The Freedom Trail is in what U.S. city?

Boston

141-In what states does the Appalachian Trail begin and end?

Northern end is in Maine and southern end is in Georgia

142-Where is the Holland Tunnel?

Connects New York & New Jersey

143-Where is the Hoover Dam?

On the border of Nevada & Arizona

144-Where are these streets located?

Rodeo Drive.......Beverly Hills

Pennsylvania Avenue........District of Columbia

Bourbon Street........New Orleans

145-What four U.S. states meet at one point?

Arizona, Colorado, Utah, New Mexico

146-In what state would you find Tampa, Orlando & Miami?

Florida

147-In what state would you find San Diego, Los Angeles & San Francisco?

California

148-Which of these states extends farthest west-New York, Pennsylvania, West Virginia, Virginia?

Virginia

149-What was the world's first National Park?

Yellowstone

150-What two countries have the largest populations?

China -- India

# Sports

1-What sport is played on a court and uses a racket, ball and net?

Tennis

2-In what country is the Wimbledon tennis championship played?

England

3-In what game do you have a racket, net and a birdie?

Badminton

4-Dorothy Hamill is associated with what sport?

Figure skating

5-What baseball team did Ted Williams play for his entire career?

Boston Red Sox

6-What sport did Lou Gehrig play?

Baseball

7-What sport is played on ice and is played with a stick and a puck?

Hockey

8-What is another name for table tennis?

Ping pong

9-Arnold Palmer is associated with what sport?

Golf

10-What sport is played in the Super bowl?

Football

11-Who was Arthur Ashe?

Tennis player

12-What does the abbreviation, "k" stand for on a baseball scorecard?

Strikeout

13-What sport did Joe DiMaggio play?

Baseball

14-What game is it that you use a ball to try to knock down ten pins?

Bowling

15-What is the Kentucky Derby?

A horse race held at Churchill Downs in Louisville Kentucky

16-What sport has the World Cup as the top prize?

Soccer

17-This man was a famous baseball player. His real name was George Herman Ruth. What name was he commonly known as?

Babe Ruth

18-Who is Bill Russell?

Basketball player –played for the Boston Celtics

19-Where do the Boston Red Sox play their home games?

Fenway Park

20-Who was Yogi Berra?

Baseball catcher-played for New York Yankees

21-What major sporting event was going on when an earthquake struck in October 1989?

World Series

# Common Bonds

1-shekel, peseta, lira, zloty, euro

Monetary units

2-noun, verb, adjective, adverb

Parts of speech

3-tetracycline, penicillin, streptomycin

Antibiotics

4-Keats, Shelley, Coleridge, Wordsworth, Byron

English romantic poets

5-Superior, Erie, Michigan, Huron, Ontario

The Great Lakes

6-legislative, judicial, executive

The three branches of the U.S. government

7-Gettysburg Address & Emancipation Proclamation

Speeches by Lincoln

8-mansard, gambrel, hipped, gabled

Styles of roof

9-Winesap, Jonathan, McIntosh

Apples

10-Jim Bowie, Davy Crockett, William Travis

Three who died at the Alamo

11-Montana, Namath, Manning

Professional football quarterbacks

12-Bing Crosby, Rudy Vallee, Mel Torme

Singers-crooners

13-William Gladstone, Winston Churchill, Benjamin Disraeli

British Prime Ministers

14-Blaze Starr, Tempest Storm, Gypsy Rose Lee

Strippers

15-Artie Shaw, Kay Kaiser, Guy Lombardo

Big Band leaders

16-Lusitania, Maine, Andrea Doria

Famous sunken ships

17-AEIOU and sometimes Y

Vowels

18-BB, Billy Jean, Martin Luther Jr.

Famous "Kings"

19-1776, 1789, 1917

Years revolutions took place. American, French Russian

20-Ionic, Corinthian, Doric

Architectural names for styles of columns

21-King, Kissinger, Mother Teresa, Elie Wiesel

Winners of Nobel Peace Prize

22-Sam Rayburn, Thomas O'Neill, Jim Wright, Tom Foley

Speakers of the U.S. House of Congress

23-"Raining cats and dogs", "Cold as ice", "Hard headed"

Clichés

24-Baushaus, Georgian, Rococo, Gothic

Architectural styles

25-Gene Autry, Roy Rogers, Tex Ritter

Singing cowboys/ films

26-Students for a Democratic Society, Weathermen, Black Panthers

Radical groups from the 1960's

27-Crab, lobster, shrimp, crayfish

Crustaceans

28-Todd, Warner, Burton, Hilton, Fisher

Husbands of Elizabeth Taylor

29-St.Thomas, St. Croix, St. John

U.S. Virgin Islands

30-Ectomorph, endomorph, mesomorph

Body types

31-Innocent, Gregory, Pius, John Paul

Popes of the Roman Catholic Church

32-Pestilence, war, famine, death

The Four Horsemen of the Apocalypse

33-Freedom from want, Freedom from fear, Freedom of worship, Freedom of speech and expression

Four freedoms – goals set forth by Franklin D. Roosevelt

34-Roboflavin, Thiamine, Ascorbic Acid

Vitamins

35-Nina, Pinta, Santa Maria

Ships of Christopher Columbus

36-Cassatt, O'Keeffe, Moses

American women artists

37-Toni Morrison, Alice Walker, Maya Angelou

Contemporary American black female writers

38-Sisley, Degas, Monet, Pissarro, Renoir, Seurat

French Impressionist Painters

39-Larry, Moe, Curley, Shemp

The "Three" Stooges

40-<u>Fibber McGee and Molly</u>, <u>The Shadow</u>, <u>The Fat Man</u>

Radio shows from the 1930's and 1940's

41-Sandra Day O'Connor, Thurgood Marshall, William Rehnquist

Supreme Court Justices

42-"The Raven", "The Gold Bug", "The Murders in the Rogue Morgue"

Stories by Edgar Allan Poe

43-Preakness, Kentucky Derby, Belmont Stakes

Horse racing's Triple Crown (3 horse races)

44-Sing Sing, Attica, Leavenworth, Alcatraz

Prisons

45-Alice, Trixie, Ralph, Ed

"The Honeymooners", the Jackie Gleason Show

46-Buddy Holly, the Big Bopper, Richie Valens

All died in a plane crash in February 1959-rock and roll singers

47-<u>The</u> <u>Sun</u> <u>also</u> <u>Rises</u>, <u>A</u> <u>Farewell</u> <u>to</u> <u>Arms</u>, <u>The</u> <u>Old</u> <u>Man</u> and <u>the</u> <u>Sea</u>

Novels by Ernest Hemingway

48-Chelsea, Soho, Piccadilly, Hyde Park, Notting Hill

Districts of London

49-The Father, the Son, the Holy Spirit

The Christian Holy Trinity

50-Billy Martin, Casey Stengel, Leo Durocher, Tommy Lasorda

Baseball managers/ coaches

51-Queens, Brooklyn, Bronx, Manhattan

Boroughs of New York City

52-Isadora Duncan, Alvin Ailey, Twyla Tharp

Dancers/ Choreographers

53-Bush, Washington, Orwell

Famous men named George

54-Orioles, Yankees, Red Sox

Major League baseball teams

55-Celtics, Lakers, Bulls

Professional Basketball teams

56-Toyota, Ford, Chevrolet

Brands of automobiles

57-Carribean, Mediterranean, Black

Names of Seas

58-Chipmunks, hedgehogs, skunks

Animals that hibernate

59-Baboon, black bear, monkey

Omnivores (eat plants & animals)

60-Platypus, echidna, dingo

Australian animals

61-Insects, crustaceans, snakes

Animals that shed their skin

62-Elephants, bats, foxes

Animals with large ears relative to their size

63-New York Giants and New York Jets

New York professional football teams

64-Stanford University, Loma Linda University, Pepperdine University

 California colleges

65-Bridgeport, New Haven, Waterbury,

Connecticut cities

66-Newark, Paterson, Trenton

New Jersey cities

67-Sioux, Des Moines, Cedar Rapids

Iowa cities

# Entertainment

1-Composer Irving Berlin wrote the campaign song, "I like Ike", for what presidential campaign?

Eisenhower

2-What singer is MOST associated with these songs?

"Minnie the Moocher"

Cab Calloway

"Mona Lisa"

Nat King Cole

"White Christmas"

Bing Crosby

"Stormy Weather"

Lena Horne

"Everybody Loves Somebody…"

Dean Martin

"I Left My Heart in San Francisco"

Tony Bennett

"Hound Dog"

Elvis Presley

3-What comedienne ended her weekly shows by tugging on her left earlobe?

Carol Burnett

4-What television network has for decades used the peacock as its logo?

NBC

5-What plump comic's television show featured the June Taylor dancers?

Jackie Gleason

6-Ben Gordy Jr. founded what record company in Detroit in 1959?

Motown Records

7-Name some Marilyn Monroe movies

Some like it Hot (1959) All about Eve (1950) Gentlemen Prefer Blondes (1953)

The Seven Year Itch (1955) Bus Stop (1956) The Misfits (1961)

8-Who was Captain Kangaroo?

The host of a children's television show

9-On what television western would you find a character named, Miss Kitty?

Gunsmoke

10-On the television show I Love Lucy what was Lucy's husband's name?

Ricky Ricardo

11-Who was Mickey Rooney's first wife?

Ava Gardner

12-In the music world he was known as the king

Elvis Presley

13-What was the name of the comedic actress that died in a plane crash in 1942?

Carole Lombard

14-What instrument was Arthur Godfrey known for playing?

Ukulele

15-Musicians --what were their last names?

Benny-----------------------Goodman

Duke--------------------------Ellington

Lawrence----------------------Welk

Guy---------------------------Lombardo

Count------------------------Basie

16-Who was Fred Astaire?

Dancer & actor

17-Who was Fred Astaire's most well known dance partner?

Ginger Rogers

18-Name a few of the conductors of the Boston Pops

John Williams, Arthur Fiedler, Keith Lockhart

19-What is the title of Bob Hope's theme song?

"Thanks for the Memories"

20-Who was the blonde pin up girl that was married to bandleader Harry James?

Bette Grable

21-Who was on the cover of the first TV guide in April 1953?

Lucille Ball's first baby-- Desi Arnez Jr.

22-Who was Liza Minelli's mother?

Judy Garland

23-Who were Stan Laurel & Oliver Hardy?

A comedy duo

24-"Happy Trails" was the theme song for what cowboy?

Roy Rogers

25-The song, "Let's dance" was the theme song of what bandleader?

Benny Goodman

26-Who was the actress that wore fruit on her head?

Carmen Miranda

27-Who was Buster Keaton?

Silent movie actor

28-In what movie would you find Rick's Café?

Casablanca

29-Who always said, "What's up doc"?

Bugs Bunny

30-What TV detective was known to say, "Who love's ya baby"?

Kojak (Telly Savalas)

31-How many freckles were on Howdy Doody's face?

48-one for each state of the union (at the time)

32-What children's TV program did Mr. Greenjeans appear on?

Captain Kangaroo

33-On what TV program would you hear the famous line, "Say the secret word and win"?

You bet your life

34-What radio serial in the 1930's featured the man of steel?

Superman

35-What were the first names of radio personalities Burns and Allen?

George and Gracie

36-In the song from the movie, Paint your Wagon, who or what was called Mariah?

The wind

37-In the story Camelot what was King Arthur's wife's name?

Guinevere

38-This husband of Elizabeth Taylor died in a plane crash in 1958

Mike Todd

39-In this movie an American Korean War veteran is programmed to be an assassin.

The Manchurian Candidate

40-What were the first names of comedians Abbot and Costello?

Bud and Lou

41-What song did Marilyn Monroe sing to John F. Kennedy on May 21, 1962 at Madison Square Garden?

"Happy Birthday"

42-What world famous rock and roll singer was born in Tupelo, Mississippi?

Elvis Presley

43-Who is Mikhail Baryshnikov?

A ballet dancer

44-What character is Christopher Reeves known for playing?

Superman

45-Who is Waylon Jennings?

Country western singer

46-Who is Harry Houdini?

A magician

47-Who is Lena Horne

Jazz singer

48- Who is Garth Brooks?

Country singer

49-What comedian hosted the Academy Award show for 18 years?

Bob Hope

50-What comedienne referred to her husband as Fang?

Phyllis Diller

51-What comedian use to clutch his chest and say, "this is the big one"?

Redd Foxx

52-Name some actors that played James Bond

Sean Connery, Roger Moore, Timothy Dalton, Pierce Brosnan, David Niven

53-What comedian always complained "that he got no respect"?

Rodney Dangerfield

54-What comedy duo asked "who's on first"?

Abbott and Costello

55-Name the four members of the Beatles

John Lennon, Paul McCartney, George Harrison, Ringo Starr

56-Who played "Carnac the Magnificent"?

Johnny Carson

57-Who was Johnny Carson's side kick?

Ed McMahon

58-What monster did Boris Karloff play?

Frankenstein

59-Who was Ernie Kovac's wife?

Edie Adams

60- What Tennessee Williams play debuted on Broadway in 1947 and promptly won the Pulitzer Prize?

A Streetcar Named Desire

61-What film producer did Sophia Loren marry in 1958?

Carlo Ponti

62-What company did Joan Crawford's husband, Alfred Steele, head?

Pepsi Cola

63-Name the Marx Brothers

Chico, Harpo, Groucho & Zeppo

64-Who starred in the Thin Man movies?

William Powell and Myrna Loy

65-Who played Dorothy in The Wizard of Oz?

Judy Garland

66-Who composed "The Four Seasons"?

Antonio Vivaldi

67-How did they die?

John Lennon-------shot

Janis Joplin---------drug overdose

Buddy Holly--------plane crash

Mama Cass Elliott--heart attack

Sal Mineo-----------stabbed

Jack Cassidy---------house fire

68-Who was Alan Funt?

Original host of TV show Candid Camera

69-Who was Al Jolson?

An American actor, singer & comedian

70-Who directed the movie "North by Northwest"?

Alfred Hitchcock

71-Who played Norman Bates in Psycho?

Anthony Perkins

72-Who directed "It's a wonderful life"?

Frank Capra

73-Who played Maria in "West Side Story"?

Natalie Wood

74-In the television show "The Golden Girls" the character played by Betty White was from what state?

Minnesota

75-Who was Joe Friday's partner on the television show "Dragnet"?

Bill Gannon

76-On the television show "Sesame Street" who was always partnered with Ernie?

Bert

77-What father and son have been given the American Film Institute lifetime achievement award?

Kirk & Michael Douglas

# Potpourri

1-What is the opposite of temporary?

Permanent

2-Who was the Lone Ranger's Indian friend?

Tonto

3-Who was Little Red Riding Hood going to visit?

Grandmother

4-Who is Donald Duck's girlfriend?

Daisy Duck

5-What is the person's title that carries a golfer's bag?

Caddie

6-In the case of a fire whose job is it to put out the fire?

Firefighter

7-What is the opposite of work?

Play

8-What is happening when you hear someone yell, "Timber"?

A tree is being cut down

9-What is a jungle?

An area of tropical vegetation

10-What is the opposite of give?

Receive

11-What is the opposite of amateur?

Professional

12-What is the opposite of sour?

Sweet

13-What is the opposite of employment?

Unemployment

14-How many stepsisters did Cinderella have?

Two

15-What type of business do we associate with Nashville?

Country music

16-What type of business do we associate with Hollywood?

Movie business

17-What state was the first to have a million dollar lottery prize October 8 1970?

New York

18-What is the national language of Brazil?

Portuguese

19-What is a gondola?

Flat bottomed Venetian rowing boat

20-What are the seven colors of the rainbow?

Red, orange, yellow, green, blue, indigo, violet

21-Complete these expressions:

Don't count your chickens……..before they hatch

Children should be seen and……..not heard

People who live in glass houses……..should not throw stones

Early to bed and early to rise……..makes a man healthy, wealthy and wise

A penny saved……..is a penny earned

March comes in like a lion and……..goes out like a lamb

Everybody talks about the weather but nobody……..does anything about it

Listen my children and you shall hear……..of the midnight ride of Paul Revere

I think that I shall never see……..a poem as lovely as a tree

Laugh and the world laughs with you……..cry and you cry alone

Time and tide wait for no……..man

Birds of a feather……..flock together

I'll do it by hook or……..by crook

Never cry over……..spilled milk

God helps those who help……..themselves

Rain, rain go away……..come again another day

One for the money……..two for the show

All good things come to……..those who wait

A stitch in time……..saves nine

To be or not to be……..that is the question

Give me liberty……..or give me death

Too many cooks spoil……..the broth

Don't look a gift horse……..in the mouth

I escaped by the skin of my……..teeth

Nothing ventured……..nothing gained

The pen is mightier than……..the sword

22-How many feet in are there in a yard?

Three

23-What is an amphibious vehicle?

A vehicle that goes on land and water

24-What does slander mean?

A false statement

25-What is libel?

A written false statement

26-What does confiscate mean?

To seize

27-What is the thin outer peel of citrus called?

Zest

28-What is Ivory Soap known for that is different than other soap?

It floats

29-What holiday is the official end of summer?

Labor Day

30-What is the chemical that gives leaves their green color?

Chlorophyll

31-Who was the greedy man in the book, A Christmas Carol?

Scrooge

32-What color is a stop sign?

Red

33-What does a solid yellow line down the middle of the road mean?

Do not cross the line-do not pass

34-Here are some brand names. What type of product is it?

Schwinn….bicycle

Dr. Pepper….carbonated soft drink

Goodrich….tires

Singer….sewing machine

Clairol….hair products

Maxwell House….coffee

Cheer….laundry detergent

Viceroy….cigarette

Studebaker….car

Schlitz….beer

Tums….antacid

35-Where would you most likely find these products?

Rumble seat….car

Landing gear….airplane

36-What are these?

Lasso….a long rope with a noose at the end

One arm bandit….slot machine for gambling

Swizzle stick….stick for mixing drinks

37-What color was the roof of the Howard Johnson Restaurants?

Orange

38-What is a marathon?

A twenty six mile foot race

39-In what town does the Boston Marathon begin?

Hopkinton

40-What do these initials stand for?

FBI……..Federal Bureau of Investigation

CIA……..Central Intelligence Agency

41-How did the Lone Ranger hide his face?

Mask

42-In what country is the yen the national currency?

Japan

43-What is the state flower of Arizona?

Saguaro cactus blossom

44-What river was Huckleberry Finn's playground?

Mississippi River

45-During cold periods some animals enter a period of inactivity. What is this physical state called?

Hibernation

46-What kind of storm is often seen in a funnel shape?

Tornado

47-What is the national flower of the U.S.?

Rose-since 1986

48-What is the study and practice of map making called?

Cartography

49-What is the largest planet in our solar system?

Jupiter

50-What is kelp?

Seaweed

51-What is a cluster of bananas called?

Hand

52-What is an ascot?

Scarf

53-What system does the gallbladder belong to?

Digestive system

54-In what part of the body is the tibia bone located?

Leg

55-Which state produces the most apples?

Washington

56-What is the most widely grown variety of apple in the U.S.?

Red delicious

57-What is a praying mantis?

Insect

58-What is sleet?

Partially frozen rain

59-What is hail?

Pellets of ice

60-What is a motorcycle?

A two wheeled vehicle powered by gasoline

61-What is the most expensive spice?

Saffron

62-What does it mean to go on strike?

Not work

63-What direction does the needle of a compass always point?

North

64-Who was Gypsy Rose Lee?

An American burlesque entertainer-know for striptease

65-What is a filibuster?

Prolonged speechmaking

66-What is penicillin?

Antibiotic drug

67-What is the jitterbug?

Dance

68-What is the state bird of Massachusetts?

Chickadee

69-What is a bobbin on a sewing machine?

Where you load the thread that will be used for the underside of stitch

70-What is a thimble?

A covering for the finger when sewing

71-What does a cappella mean?

Singing without an instrument

72-What does a la carte mean?

Ordering items individually

73-What does a la mode mean?

Served with ice cream—in fashion it means the current style

74-What is a mimosa?

A cocktail with orange juice and champagne

75-What is a harmonica?

An instrument

76-What is a swamp?

A wetland

77-What is an abbey?

A Christian monastery or convent

78-How many letters are there in the English language alphabet?

Twenty six

79-Emmett Kelly became famous as a sad faced what?

Clown

80-What kind of boat is used to carry people, cars & freight?

Ferry

81-How many seasons are there in a year?

Four—winter, spring, summer & fall

82-What is the name of the planet we live on?

Earth

83-What is a kayak?

A boat

84-What are the five senses?

Hearing, sight, smell, taste & touch

85-What type of book is Agatha Christie famous for writing?

Detective / mystery

86-How many inches are there in a foot?

Twelve

87-What is a jockey?

A person who rides a horse in a race

88-What cartoon character loved Olive Oyl and spinach?

Popeye

89-How many pints are there in a quart?

Two

90-How many quarts are there in a gallon?

Four

91-What food chain used the phrase "where's the beef"?

Wendy's

92-What is the day after Halloween called?

All saints day

93-What is a podiatrist?

A doctor that takes care of the feet

94-What is Graceland?

The estate of Elvis Presley

95-What design is on the Canadian flag?

Maple leaf

96-What is a flounder?

A type of flatfish

97-Where did the famous "Tea Party" occur in 1773?

Boston

98-What is fresco?

A painting on a wall or ceiling

99-Which planet is the "red planet"?

Mars

100-Where is Walden Pond?

Concord, Massachusetts

101-Who sculpted the "Gates of Paradise"?

Lorenzo Ghiberti

102-What artist died the same year that Shakespeare was born?

Michelangelo (1564)

103-What film did the AFI rank as the number 1 film of the twentieth century?

"Citizen Kane"

104-What was the first state to join the Confederacy?

South Carolina

105-Alexander Graham Bell also invented this device first used after the assassination of President James Garfield

Metal detector

106-What country was Adolf Hitler born in?

Austria-Hungary

107-What was the first grocery chain in the United States?

A & P

108-How many states have 4 letter names?

3- Iowa, Ohio & Utah

109-In what sport do you hear the terms woods and irons?

Golf

110-How many innings are in a major league baseball game?

Nine

111-In basketball what is traveling?

Moving pivot foot or taking too many steps

112-In what state is the Football Hall of Fame?

Ohio

113-What PGA player made a hole in one on a par 4?

Andrew Magee

114-What athlete has appeared on the cover of Sports Illustrated the most times?

Michael Jordan

115-The Miracle on Ice in the 1980 Olympics was a hockey game played by what two countries?

United States & Soviet Union

116-Who did George H.W. Bush call a card carrying member of the ACLU?

Michael Dukakis

# Bible

1-Who killed Goliath with a sling and a stone?

David (1 Samuel 17:49-51)

2-What would be a sign to the shepherds that a savior was born?

A baby wrapped in cloths and lying in a manger (Luke 2:12)

3-Anyone who touches a dead body was considered unclean for how long?

7 days (Numbers 19:11)

4-Which one of Jesus' disciples had been a disciple of John the Baptist?

Andrew (John 1:40)

5-Who died when the water flowed back in the parted red sea?

The Egyptians (Exodus 14:26-28)

6-What happened to Saul on his way to Damascus after Jesus finished speaking to him?

He was completely blind (Acts 9: 8-9)

7-On what day did the dry ground appear?

The third day (Genesis 1:9)

8-What role did Onesiphorus play in the Apostle Paul's life?

He ministered to his needs (2 Timothy 1: 16-18)

9-What did the widow make for the prophet Elijah?

Bread (1 Kings 17:13)

10-What event brought Mary and Joseph to Bethlehem?

Census (Luke 2:4-5)

11-What was Jesus doing when a storm came up on the Sea of Galilee?

Sleeping (Matthew 8:23-27)

12-Who said, can anything good come out of Nazareth?

Nathanael (John 1:46)

13-Jeremiah was born only a few miles north of Jerusalem, in what city?

Anathoth (Jeremiah 1:1)

14-What did Moses' staff turn into?

Snake (Exodus 4:2-3)

15-Who went to Saul and prayed that he might regain his sight and be filled with the Holy Spirit?

Ananias (Acts 9:17)

16-Who was the first murder victim in the Bible?

Abel—killed by Cain (Genesis 4:8)

17-Who was the oldest man in the Bible?

Methuselah – 969 years (Genesis 5:27)

18-In Revelation the new city of Jerusalem was made of what?

Pure gold (Revelation 21:18)

19-What city's walls fell when trumpets sounded and people shouted?

Jericho (Joshua 6: 20)

20-To whom did Jesus say, "Get behind me Satan"?

Peter (Matthew 16:23)

21-Where was Jesus baptized?

Jordan River (Matthew 3:13)

22-Who saw the back of God, since no one could see God's face and live?

Moses (Exodus 33: 20-23)

23-The people of Israel were permitted to eat only fish with what physical characteristics?

Fins and scales (Leviticus 11:12)

24-Samson's strength was connected with what part of his body?

Hair (Judges 16:19)

25-How did Judas die?

He hung himself (Matthew 27: 3-5)

26-Who poured expensive perfume on Jesus' feet?

Mary (John 12: 3)

27-In Jeremiah's day the influence of the Canaanite god was still strong-which god?

Baal (Jeremiah 2: 8)

28-How were the Israelites spared the plagues?

Blood displayed on their doors (Exodus 12:7)

29-How did Saul escape from the angry Jews in Damascus?

His followers took him at night and lowered him in a basket through an opening in a wall

(Acts 9:25)

30-Noah sent two types of birds from the ark. What types of birds were they?

Raven and dove (Genesis 8:7-8)

31-The Old Testament law is described in the Bible as what?

Law of Moses (Joshua 8:32)

32-"In the same way, faith by itself, if not accompanied by_____ is dead"

Action (James 2:17)

33-What type of work did Matthew do before he was a disciple?

Tax collector (Matthew 9: 9)

34-Who looked for Jesus for three days in Jerusalem?

Mary and Joseph (Luke 2:46)

35-Christ said to render to Caesar that which is Caesar's. What did he say we should render to God?

Things that are God's (Luke 20: 25)

36-Who attempted to kill Jeremiah for preaching God's message of destruction?

The men of Anathoth (Jeremiah 11: 18-23)

37-On what mountain did Moses receive the Ten Commandments?

Mt. Sinai (Exodus 19)

38-What did Saul tell Elymas the sorcerer that God would do to him for perverting the truth?

Strike him blind (Acts 13:8-11)

39-After Noah built the ark how many days was the earth flooded?

150 days (Genesis 7:24)

40 In the book of Revelation how many were sealed from the tribes of Israel?

144,000 (Revelation 7:4)

41-Complete this phrase---Take the helmet of salvation, and the sword of the Spirit------which is the word of God   (Ephesians 6:17)

42-Elisha purified a pot of stew that had been poisoned with what?

Wild gourds (2 Kings 4: 38-41)

43-To whom did Paul write, "Do your best to come before winter"?

Timothy (2 Timothy 4:21)

44-What was Simon Peter's brother's name?

Andrew (Matthew 4:18)

45-Job cursed the day-- then what did he wish?

That he had never been born (Job 3:1-3)

46-Who did the people of Lystra think Paul and Barnabas were?

Hermes and Zeus (Acts 14: 11-12)

47-How many years after the flood did Noah live?

350 Years (Genesis 9:28)

48-What was an acceptable burnt offering for the Israelites to sacrifice?

A dove or a young pigeon (Leviticus 1:14)

49-Who was the woman that tricked Samson into telling her the secret of his strength?

 Delilah (Judges 16:4-19)

50-Who was Jonah?

A minor prophet, he tried to flee from the Lord. He was swallowed by a great fish and was in the fish for 3 days. (Jonah 1)

51-Who gave Solomon the plan for the temple?

King David, his father (1 Chronicles 28: 11)

52-Is this actually from the Bible? "Do not judge or you too will be judged"

Yes (Matthew 7:1)

53-What was the Apostle Peter's original name?

Simon (John 1: 42)

54-How many sons and daughters did Job father after his sufferings?

7 sons and 3 daughters (Job 42: 13)

55-Why were Paul and Silas thrown into a prison?

For casting an evil spirit out of a slave girl (Acts 16: 16-23)

56-How many years did Noah live in total?

950 (Genesis 9: 29)

57-Where did the Israelites set up twelve stones taken from the river as a memorial to their crossing of the Jordan?

Gilgal (Joshua 4:19-24)

58-Who was taken to heaven in a whirlwind?

Elijah (2 Kings 2:11)

59-The Lord knows how to rescue the --------out of temptations.

Godly (2 Peter 2: 9)

60-Who sat on a sack cloth among the rocks during harvest to prevent birds from devouring her dead sons who had been hanged?

Rizpah (2 Samuel 21: 8-10)

61-Who woke up under a tree and found an angel had cooked food for him?

Elijah (1 Kings 19: 1-8)

62-Is this actually from the Bible? "Do unto others as you would have them do unto you"

Yes (Matthew 7:12)

63-Who gives us the power to get wealth?

God (Deuteronomy 8: 18)

64-Who in the Bible was over 9 feet tall?

Goliath (1 Samuel 17:4)

65-It is written, that man shall not live by--------alone, but by every word of God.

bread (Luke 4: 4)

66-Who is the Lamb of God?

Jesus (John 1: 29)

67-How much longer did Job live after his sufferings?

140 years (Job 42: 16-17)

68-What is the name of the mountain where the burning bush is located-where God spoke to Moses?

Horeb (Exodus 3:1-2)

69-Paul was shipwrecked on what island on his way to Rome?

Malta (Acts 28: 1)

70-The Ark of the Covenant was carried around and around what city?

Jericho (Joshua 6)

71-Who saw a vision concerning Judah and Jerusalem in the days of Uzziah, Jotham, Ahaz and Hezekiah, kings of Judah?

Isaiah (Isaiah 1:1)

72-An angel appeared to him in a dream and assured him that his wife had not been unfaithful to him.

Joseph (Matthew 1: 20-21)

73-King Ahab asked Naboth for what? So he could turn it into what?

His vineyard--------into a vegetable garden (1 Kings 21:2)

74-What was placed in the Ark of the Covenant along with the golden pot that had manna and Aaron's rod that budded?

The stone tablets of the covenant (Hebrews 9:4)

75-Did Jesus do away with capital punishment?

No (Matthew 5: 17-21)

76-What percent of their increase were the Israelites commanded to tithe to God?

10 % (Deuteronomy 14: 22-29)

77-The Sermon on the Mount can be found in which book of the Bible?

Matthew

78-Fill in the blank---------

Blessed are the --------: for they will be called children of God.

peacemakers (Matthew 5:9)

Blessed are the--------: for they will be shown mercy.

merciful (Matthew 5:7)

Blessed are the--------: for they will inherit the earth.

meek (Matthew 5:5)

Blessed are the--------: for they will see God.

pure in heart (Matthew 5:8)

Blessed are those--------: for they will be comforted.

who mourn   (Matthew 5:4)

Blessed are those--------: for theirs is the Kingdom of Heaven

who are persecuted because of their righteousness (Matthew 5: 10)

Blessed are those--------: for they will be filled.

who hunger and thirst for righteousness (Matthew 5:6)

79-Christ said he came to--------: the law.

fulfill (Matthew 5:17)

80-Judging from his occupation, who would you most likely find in a hospital?

Luke –physician (Colossians 4:14)

81-What did Paul call the Galatians?

Foolish (Galatians 3:1)

82-Which days of creation are described in Genesis?

The first six (Genesis 1)

83-Who did Ruth marry after her first husband died?

Boaz (Ruth 4: 9-10)

84-What prisoner was released in Jesus' place?

Barabbas (Matthew 27: 26)

85-Paul healed Publius' father of what?

Fever and dysentery (Acts 28:8)

86-Jewish boys were circumcised when they were how old?

Eight days (Leviticus 12:1-3)

87-What did John the Baptist eat in the wilderness?

Locusts and wild honey (Matthew 3: 4)

88-What prophetess once lead Israel?

Deborah (Judges 4:4)

89-What did the chief priests buy with the money that Judas returned to them?

A potter's field as a burial place for foreigners (Matthew 27: 7)

90-What does Proverbs say is like merchant ships bringing food from afar?

A wife of noble character (Proverbs 31: 10-14)

91-What were the doors to the priest's court and the great court overlaid with?

Bronze (2 Chronicles 4: 9)

92-Nebuchadnezzar was king of what city?

Babylon (Daniel 1:1)

93-To whom did Jesus say, "Man does not live on bread alone"?

The devil (Matthew 4:4)

94-Who dwelt by the Kerith Ravine and was fed by ravens?

Elijah (1 Kings 17: 1-6)

95-Father, if you are willing, take this--------from me: yet not my will, but yours be done

cup (Luke 22: 42)

96-In what land did Job live?

Uz (Job 1: 1)

97-How many times did Peter think one should be willing to forgive his neighbor?

Up to seven times (Matthew 18:21)

98-What was the cost of David's sin with Bathsheba?

Their first born would die (2 Samuel 12: 14-19)

99-In Genesis who named the animals?

God (Genesis 1)

100-When Moses struck the Nile River with his staff what did the water turn into?

Blood (Exodus 7:20)

101-An angel of the Lord struck this ruler down because he did not give glory to God

Herod (Acts 12: 21-23)

102-Who found honey inside the body of a dead lion?

Samson (Judges 14:5-9)

103-What does Emmanuel mean?

God with us (Matthew 1:23)

104-Aaron threw his staff on the ground and what did it become?

Snake (Exodus 7:9)

105-What very large Philistine died from a blow to the head from a rock?

Goliath (1 Samuel 17:50-51)

106-In the Book of Revelation, how many elders were seated around the throne in Heaven?

24 (Revelation 4:4)

107-How many lampstands of gold did Solomon have set in the temple?

10 (2 Chronicles 4:7)

108-Who attempted to comfort Job?

His friends (Job 2: 11-13)

109-What kind of seed did Jesus use to illustrate the Kingdom of Heaven?

Mustard seed (Matthew 13: 31)

110-The Lord said to Jeremiah that he would break Jerusalem as what is broken?

A potter's jar (Jeremiah 19:11)

111-What did ravens bring to Elijah in the wilderness?

Bread and meat (1 Kings 17:6)

112-According to the Apostle Paul, what is the problem with loving money?

The love of money is a root of all kinds of evil (1 Timothy 6:10)

113-Who stayed on the mountain for 40 days and 40 nights without eating or drinking?

Moses (Deuteronomy 9:9)

114-Who asked, "How can a man be born when he is old"?

Nicodemus (John 3:4)

Fill in the blank

115-Father--------them, for they do not know what they are doing

forgive (Luke 23:34)

116-How did David's son Absalom die?

Three daggers thrust into his heart (2 Samuel 18:14)

117-When they came to Perga, who left Paul's company and returned to Jerusalem?

John (Acts 13:13)

118-In the Book of Proverbs, what is like a kiss on the lips?

An honest answer (Proverbs 24:26)

119-To what city did the Lord ask Jonah to go?

Nineveh (Jonah 1:1-2)

Fill in the blanks

120-"It is easier for a --------to go through the eye of a--------than for a rich man to enter the kingdom of God.

camel--------needle (Matthew 19:24)

121-How old was David when he first began to reign over Judah?

30 years old (2 Samuel 5:4)

122-In the Book of 2 Peter what does God do to the angels that sinned?

Put them in gloomy dungeons to be held for judgment (2 Peter 2:4)

123-Who had a dream about an image with a head of gold, arms of silver and a belly of bronze?

Nebuchadnezzar (Daniel 2: 28-33)

124-What was Adam doing when God made Eve?

Sleeping (Genesis 2:21)

125-How did Judas identify Jesus for the soldiers?

He kissed him (Matthew 26:49)

126-Where was Jesus praying when he was arrested?

Garden of Gethsemane (Matthew 26: 36-50)

127-At the dedication of the Temple, when Solomon had ended his prayer to the Lord, what happened?

Fire came down from Heaven and consumed the burnt offering and the sacrifices and the Glory of the Lord filled the Temple. (2 Chronicles 7:1)

128-After crossing the Red Sea, Israel camped in Elim where there were 70 of what kind of tree?

Palm (Exodus 15:27)

129-Who became a pillar of salt as punishment for looking back at Sodom and Gomorrah?

Lot's wife (Genesis 19:26)

130-What time of year was it when Naomi returned to her homeland with Ruth?

Barley harvest season (Ruth 1:22)

131-Job's friends kept vigil with him in silence for how long?

7 days (Job 2:13)

132-The two pillars of the temple were named----

Jakin (south) and Boaz (north) (1 Kings 7:21)

133-How did the writer of the book of Hebrews refer to angels?

Ministering spirits (Hebrews 1:14)

134-According to God's law, there is a difference between killing a person and murdering a person---is this true or false?

True (Deuteronomy 19: 1-13)

135-Who said, "It is more blessed to give than to receive"?

Jesus (Acts 20:35)

135-Saul was present at the stoning of what early disciple of Jesus?

Stephen (Acts 7:57-59)

136-What kind of crown was placed on Jesus' head?

Crown of thorns (Matthew 27:29)

137-Who was chosen by the other eleven Apostles to replace Judas?

Matthias (Acts 1:26)

138-What are the ten plagues of Egypt?

Transformed the Nile River into blood

Covered the land with frogs

Changed dust to gnats

Produced swarms of flies

Massacred the Egyptian livestock

Festered boils on all the Egyptian people and animals

Sent down a severe hailstorm

Covered the land with locusts

Put Egypt in total darkness for 3 days

God struck down the Egyptian first born sons (Exodus 7-11)

139-What three gifts did the Magi present to the baby Jesus?

Gold, frankincense & myrrh (Matthew 2:11)

140-Who was accused of bringing Greeks into the Temple of God?

Paul (Acts 21:28-29)

141-Where should we store our treasures?

In Heaven (Matthew 6:19-20)

142-On what mountain did Noah's Ark land?

Mount Ararat (Genesis 8:4)

143-What caused the death of Job's children?

A violent wind storm (Job 1: 19)

144-When David became old why does scripture record that his servants covered him with blankets?

He could not get warm (1 Kings 1:1)

145-Why did Moses flee to the land of Midian?

He had killed an Egyptian and feared for his life (Exodus 2: 14-15)

146-How old was Moses when he died?

120 years old (Deuteronomy 34: 7)

147-Who introduced Peter to Jesus?

Andrew (John 1: 40-42)

148-Which angel appeared to Mary?

Gabriel (Luke 1:26-28)

149-What kind of event was Jesus attending when he changed water into wine?

Wedding (John 2: 1-10)

150-What king sent the Magi to find the baby Jesus?

King Herod (Matthew 2: 7-8)

151-Did this expression actually come from the Bible? "The fear of the Lord is the beginning of knowledge"?

True (Proverbs 1:7)

152-Who spoke these words just before he died? "It is finished"

Jesus (John 19: 30)

153-Once the Israelites began living with and marrying other nations what else began to happen?

They began to serve their gods.  (Judges 3:6)

154-Which river runs between the Sea of Galilee and the Dead Sea?

The River Jordan (Deuteronomy 3:17)

155-According to scripture what caused Solomon to turn his heart from God to follow other gods?

His many wives from other nations (1Kings 11:4)

156-Where did Paul write the book of Philippians?

Prison (Philippians)

157-Where in the Bible is this verse found? eye for eye, tooth for tooth, hand for hand, foot for foot

Exodus (Exodus 21:24)

158-What was the purpose of sacrificing burnt offerings?

God received it as atonement for sin. (Leviticus 1:4)

159-As the Israelites were about to enter the Promised Land how many nations did God promise to give to them?

Seven (Deuteronomy 7:1-2)

160-God promised Abraham "I will make your descendants as the -----------

of the earth"

dust (Genesis 13:16)

161-Saul met a band of prophets coming down from a place of worship-what instruments were they playing?

Harp, tambourine, flute & lyre (1 Samuel 10: 5)

162-Who is the bread of life?

Jesus (John 6: 48-51)

163-Saul was how old when he became king and how long did he reign?

30 years old and he reigned for 42 years (1 Samuel 13:1)

164-While at Gilgal waiting for Samuel, what did Saul do that angered Samuel?

He sacrificed the burnt offerings (1 Samuel 13:7-9)

165-What was Moses' father-in-law's name?

Jethro, the priest of Midian (Exodus 18:1)

Made in the USA
Coppell, TX
27 February 2020